W9-CKI-022

# SEE HOW THEY GROW

# OWL

## photographed by
## KIM TAYLOR

DORLING KINDERSLEY

London • New York • Stuttgart

# Just hatched

I am a barn owl chick. I am just hatching out of my eggshell.

I chip around the shell and push myself free.

**A DORLING KINDERSLEY BOOK**

**Written and edited by** Mary Ling
**Art Editor** Helen Senior
**Production** Louise Barratt
**Illustrator** Jane Cradock-Watson
**Additional photography** Steve Gorton

First published in Great Britain in 1992 by
Dorling Kindersley Limited, 9 Henrietta Street, London WC2E 8PS

Reprinted 1993

Copyright © 1992 Dorling Kindersley Limited, London

All rights reserved. No part of this publication may be reproduced, stored
in a retrieval system, or transmitted in any form or by any means,
electronic, mechanical, photocopying, recording or otherwise, without the
prior permission of the copyright owner.

A CIP catalogue record for this book is available
from the British Library

ISBN 0-86318-865-6

Colour reproduction by J. Film Ltd, Singapore
Printed in Italy by L.E.G.O.

This is my mother.
I will snuggle under
her soft feathers to
keep myself warm.

# Little brother

I am one week old. This is my little brother. He has just hatched.

Mum watches over us.
She hisses when
there is danger.
We run and hide
under her wings.

Sometimes we get very
tired. Shhh! My little
brother is sleeping.

# Time to eat

I am three weeks old today.
I can see now. My legs are strong
enough to walk and jump.

My brother
and I are
hungry. Dad
is hunting for
our supper.

Look! Here is
Dad. He brings
us lots of lovely
things to eat.

# Fluff to feathers

I am six weeks old. My wing feathers are starting to grow through my fluffy white down.

I look very handsome, just like my Dad.

# Out of the nest

I am eight weeks old and my feathers are really growing. Now I am ready to go out of the nest.

I twist and turn my head when I hear sounds around me that I do not know.

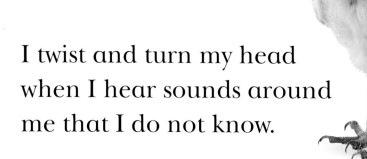

My wings get stronger
every day. I practise flying
from branch to branch.

# Flying high

I am ten weeks old.
Now I can explore
on my own.

Each day I fly higher
and higher into the air.

When I reach the
end of my journey,
I land carefully.

17

# On the wing

I am twelve weeks old
and almost fully
grown. I hunt for my
own food now.

I glide silently through
the air on my long wings.

# See how I grew

Just hatched

One week old

Three weeks old     Six weeks old     Eight weeks old

Ten weeks old　　　　Twelve weeks old